PIANO / VOCAL / GUITAR

CROONERS

EIGHTY-FOUR SONGS BY TWENTY-EIGHT MARVEL___ ___ISTS

2 CONTENTS

4 SINGER INDEX

6 THE CROONERS

16 THE SONGS

On the cover:
Bobby Darin, Billy Eckstine,
Brook Benton, Vic Damone,
Mel Tormé, Bing Crosby, Tony Martin

Photos of Fred Astaire, Hoagy Carmichael, Perry Como, Bing Crosby, Vic Damone,
Eddie Fisher, Johnny Hartman, Dick Haymes, Jack Jones, Tony Martin, Johnny Mercer, Matt Monroe,
Vaughn Monroe, Frank Sinatra, Mel Tormé, Bobby Vinton
courtesy of Photofest

Photos of Tony Bennett, Brook Benton, Pat Boone, Nat "King" Cole, Bobby Darin, Sammy Davis Jr.,
Billy Eckstine, Frankie Laine, Dean Martin, Johnny Mathis, Johnnie Ray, Joe Williams
courtesy of William "PoPsie" Randolph
www.PoPsiePhotos.com

ISBN 978-1-4234-6366-5

HAL•LEONARD®
CORPORATION

7777 W. BLUEMOUND RD. P.O. BOX 13819 MILWAUKEE, WI 53213

Visit Hal Leonard Online at
www.halleonard.com

CONTENTS

SINGER INDEX

CROONERS

THE BIOGRAPHIES

FRED ASTAIRE
(1899-1987)

Over the course of his 76-year career as a dancer, choreographer, singer and actor, Fred Astaire became a household name in the United States. Born Frederick Austerlitz in Omaha, Astaire collected two Academy Awards®, two Emmy® Awards, three Golden Globes® and a long list of other honors and awards. The debonair Astaire was paired with elegant actress, dancer and singer Ginger Rogers in ten films. He introduced "Cheek to Cheek" while dancing with Rogers in *Top Hat* in 1935. He sang "The Way You Look Tonight," while sitting at a piano in the 1936 film *Swing Time*, only to turn and see Rogers with her hair covered in shampoo. Rogers was dancing with someone else when Astaire sang "Change Partners" in the 1938 film *Carefree*. Despite his unforgettable film performances and recordings, Astaire always claimed he couldn't sing.

TONY BENNETT
(B. 1926)

Born Anthony Dominick Benedetto in Queens, New York, Tony Bennett is the quintessential comeback kid. The World War II U.S. Army veteran got his big break in 1949 thanks to Pearl Bailey and Bob Hope. A lifelong civil rights activist, Bennett developed a unique interpretive style that imitated the playing of some of the best jazz musicians of his day. He won his first GRAMMY® in 1962. When the Beatles and the groups that followed them took over the 1960s pop scene, Bennett's career faltered. After Bennett's drug overdose in 1979, his son Danny took over management of his father's career, creating a new image for him. The singer's class act found a new audience, winning him twelve GRAMMYs from 1992 to 2006, and a Lifetime Achievement GRAMMY in 2001. He made cameo appearances as himself in films and on television, and has won Emmy® Awards for his work on A&E and PBS. Bennett is also an accomplished visual artist, painting under the name Benedetto.

BROOK BENTON
(1931-1988)

Born in Camden, South Carolina, Benjamin Franklin Peay began singing gospel as a teenager. He established himself as a songwriter and record producer in the 1950s and recorded a few songs. His big break as a singer came in 1959 with the song "It's Just a Matter of Time," which made it to #3 on the *Billboard* Hot 100 chart and #1 on the R&B chart. In addition to solo hits, Benton put "Baby (You've Got What It Takes)" on the charts in a recording with singer Dinah Washington. His smooth baritone voice landed more than fifty songs on the rock, pop and R&B charts in the late 1950s and early 1960s, until the Beatles and other British Invasion bands took over the charts. Benton made a comeback in 1970 with the song "Rainy Night in Georgia."

PAT BOONE
(B. 1934)

Charles Eugene Boone has been tagged by *Billboard* magazine as the "second biggest-charting artist of the late 1950s," behind Elvis. Born in Jacksonville, Florida and raised in Nashville, Boone sported a clean-cut, wholesome image on and off the stage. A born-again Christian, he began recording gospel music in the late 1950s, turning his focus to this genre some years later. Boone is a member of the Gospel Music Hall of Fame. Over the course of his career, Boone put sixty hits on the U.S. charts, hitting #1 six times. He took "I Almost Lost My Mind" to #1 in 1956, and "Love Letters in the Sand" to the top spot in 1957, where it stayed for five weeks. Boone continued his public life as a preacher, motivational speaker and television personality.

HOAGY CARMICHAEL
(1899-1981)

Named for a circus act, Hoagland "Hoagy" Howard Carmichael was born in Bloomington, Indiana. He learned to play the piano from his mother, who played for silent films and parties. Carmichael earned a law degree but left it behind, moving to New York City in 1929 to become a musician. He had some success with "Rockin' Chair," for which he wrote music and lyrics, but was thinking of getting out of music when "Georgia on My Mind" changed his mind. Thought of as one of the most creative songwriters in the business, Carmichael moved to Hollywood in 1936, where he continued to write songs and launched an acting career. He was inducted into the Songwriters Hall of Fame in 1971. Despite many successful recordings, Carmichael often said he had "Wabash fog and sycamore twigs" in his throat.

NAT "KING" COLE
(1919-1965)

Born in Alabama and raised in Chicago, Nathaniel Adams Coles was nicknamed "King" in 1937 by a Los Angeles nightclub owner. Although Cole's smooth, mellow voice put sixty songs in the Top 30 between 1943 and 1954, he also led a jazz trio from the piano for many years. He fought for equal rights and became the first African-American performer to have his own radio program and later, to host a television show. In 1956, while playing in Montgomery, Cole was attacked onstage by a group of white supremacists. He never played in the South again. Cole received a GRAMMY in 1959 and a posthumous Lifetime Achievement GRAMMY in 1990. He was inducted posthumously into the Rock and Roll Hall of Fame in 2000, in the "Early Influence" category.

PERRY COMO
(1912-2001)

Born near Pittsburgh, Pierino Ronald Como ran a barbershop while attending high school. He sang at weddings and parties on the side. In 1933 he won a job with Freddie Carlone's band and married his high school sweetheart. Both music and the marriage proved lifelong commitments. Como became one of the best-loved American singers and television personalities of his era. He put 127 songs into the Top 30, thirteen of them hitting the #1 spot, during his six-decade career. He took music to television (NBC) in 1948, moving to CBS two years later with a fifteen-minute show seen after the evening news three nights per week. He became the highest paid television performer of the time, winning a ratings battle with Jackie Gleason. Como won a GRAMMY in 1958, the first year of the awards, and a posthumous Lifetime Achievement GRAMMY in 2002.

BING CROSBY
(1903-1977)

Born in Tacoma, Washington, Harry Lillis Crosby spent twenty years as the reigning king of three entertainment genres: recordings, radio and film. He is remembered as the most often electronically recorded voice in history. Known by his childhood nickname, he became one of the most popular musical acts in history, and was voted the most admired man alive in the late 1940s. Crosby, who wanted to be a lawyer, was led into show business by a mail-order drum set. After his big break in 1926, from bandleader Paul Whiteman, Crosby worked with Bix Beiderbecke, Jack Teagarden, Hoagy Carmichael and the Dorseys, among others. His smooth-as-silk sound put four hundred songs on the pop charts. In 1962, Crosby, whose hits predated the GRAMMY awards, became the first recipient of a Lifetime Achievement GRAMMY. He won an Academy Award® in 1944.

VIC DAMONE
(B. 1928)

Born in Brooklyn, Vito Rocco Farinola was working as a theater usher in Manhattan when he got a chance to sing for Perry Como. Como became a mentor to the young singer, introducing and referring him to people in the business. Taking his mother's maiden name as his stage name, a nineteen-year-old Damone won a talent search on *Arthur Godfrey's Talent Scouts* in 1947. Within a few months he had a recording contract, and just a year later he had a weekly radio show. Over the years he appeared in movies and on television, released numerous recordings on several labels, and became a Vegas nightclub regular. Frank Sinatra once commented on Damone's velvety sound, saying he had "the best set of pipes in the business."

BOBBY DARIN
(1936-1973)

Bronx-born Walden Robert Cassotto lost his father as an infant and was raised on welfare by his British mother. Rheumatic fever, at age eight, weakened Darin's heart and caused his death at age thirty-seven. The singer/songwriter launched his career after one year of college, scoring a multi-million-selling hit in 1959 with his ballad "Dream Lover." Darin developed a close friendship with comedian, actor and writer George Burns, referring to him as the father he never had. In the course of his short life, Darin appeared in thirteen films, owned a publishing business, recorded with Johnny Mercer, had his own television variety show and was married to Sandra Dee for several years. He won two GRAMMY awards in 1959, was inducted into the Rock & Roll Hall of Fame in 1990 and the Songwriters Hall of Fame in 1999.

SAMMY DAVIS JR. (1925-1990)

Born in New York City, Samuel George Davis, Jr. began his entertaining career playing vaudeville with his father. Davis, who lost his left eye in a 1954 car accident, was known as a dancer, singer and all-around entertainer. He was the only African-American in Frank Sinatra's Rat Pack. Davis' recordings climbed high on several charts, including "What Kind of Fool Am I?" which hit #6 on the Billboard Easy Listening chart and #17 on the Billboard Hot 100 chart. He appeared in films and on television, played nightclubs and made hit records. Davis was nominated for a Golden Globe® and for several Emmy® Awards, including one for an appearance on *The Cosby Show* and one for *The Sammy Davis Jr.'s 60th Anniversary Celebration* in 1990. Davis was awarded a posthumous GRAMMY Lifetime Achievement Award in 2001.

BILLY ECKSTINE (1914-1993)

Known by many in the business as "Mr. B.," Billy Eckstine launched his career when he won an amateur singing contest in 1930. He was born William Clarence Eckstein in Pittsburg, and was raised in Washington, D.C. He changed the spelling of his last name because a club owner thought it looked "too Jewish." He was committed to bebop and helped build the careers of Charlie Parker, Sarah Vaughan, Dizzy Gillespie, Miles Davis and others. Although he was also a trumpeter and a snappy dresser who patented the Mr. B. Collar, he is best remembered for his rich, seamless, baritone voice and polished deliveries. That smooth sound, and the ballad singing he turned to when popular taste swung away from big bands, made him the first African-American romantic male in the pop music industry. He was a favorite guest on late night and variety television shows like *The Tonight Show* and *The Dean Martin Show*.

EDDIE FISHER (B. 1928)

The son of Russian, Jewish immigrants, Edwin Jack Fisher was born in Philadelphia. A talented child, he entered, and often won, amateur contests. He left high school during his senior year to chase his dream of singing. He was drafted and spent a year in Korea before becoming the official vocal soloist for Pershing's Own United States Army Band. A close friend and protégé of performer Eddie Cantor, Fisher became a nightclub performer after his Army stint and hosted television variety shows. He was married five times, once to Elizabeth Taylor and once to Debbie Reynolds. He and Reynolds are the parents of actress Carrie Fisher (Princess Leia in the original *Star Wars* trilogy). He took "Oh! My Pa-pa" to the top of the pop charts in 1953, shortly before rock took over.

JOHNNY HARTMAN
(1923-1983)

Chicago native John Maurice Hartman was dubbed the "quintessential romantic balladeer" in a National Public Radio profile. He sang with Dizzy Gillespie's big band, recorded with Earl Hines, made numerous recordings and did spectacular work with John Coltrane's quartet. He sang with an exceptionally rich, polished, baritone voice, creating an absolutely distinctive, smooth sound and conveying tremendous emotion through elegant nuances. But Hartman's name and sound were largely unknown outside jazz circles during his lifetime. His 1980 album *Once in Every Life* earned him a GRAMMY nomination. Hartman was inducted into the Big Band Hall of Fame three years after his death. His music found a new, much broader audience twelve years after his death, when director Clint Eastwood included several of his songs in his 1995 film *The Bridges of Madison County*.

DICK HAYMES
(1916-1980)

One of the most popular pop singers of the 1940s, Dick Haymes was born in Buenos Aires to parents of Scottish and Irish descent. He lived in Paris for a time as a child, moving to New York with his mother during the Depression. Haymes set out for Hollywood in 1933, where he tried songwriting and formed a short-lived band. In 1939 he was hired to sing with Harry James' band, a job he kept for nearly a decade. He also sang with the Benny Goodman and Tommy Dorsey bands, building a successful career that included radio, film and recordings. The calm, satin sound of Haymes' baritone voice gave no clue to the turmoil that filled his personal life, including financial troubles and six marriages.

JACK JONES
(B. 1938)

Born in Hollywood to the show business family of actor Allan Jones and actress Irene Hervey, singer Jack Jones was just nineteen when he began his career in his father's Vegas act. After only three weeks Jones struck out on his own, working odd jobs to support his singing ambitions. He made a couple of recordings, but was still working as a filling station attendant when he first heard one of his own songs on the radio of a stranger's car. Mel Tormé called Jones "one of the greatest 'pure' singers in the world." Jones' smooth, tenor voice is familiar to millions, thanks to his recording of the theme song for the television series *The Love Boat*. Jones won two GRAMMY Awards, in 1961 and 1963, one of them for his recording of "Lollipops and Roses."

FRANKIE LAINE
(1913-2007)

Starting out as a marathon dancer at age seventeen, Francesco Paolo LoVecchio set the all-time marathon dance record in Atlantic City, dancing 3,501 hours over 145 consecutive days. The son of Sicilian immigrants, he then tried his luck at singing, capturing the interest and assistance of jazz musician and songwriter Hoagy Carmichael. His big break came in 1947, with a cover recording of "That's My Desire." He scored twenty-one gold records and performed in several films, including Mel Brooks' *Blazing Saddles*. His recording of the theme song for the television series *Rawhide* became one of the most popular television theme songs of all time. Laine's recording of "I Believe" was at #1 on the U.K. singles chart three times, for a total of eighteen weeks, more weeks than any other single before or since.

DEAN MARTIN
(1917-1995)

Dino Paul Crocetti dropped out of an Ohio high school to work in illegal gambling and bootlegging establishments on his way to becoming one of the most famous entertainers of the 1950s and '60s. Although Martin did well on the nightclub circuit, his big break came when he appeared as a duo with Jerry Lewis in 1946. The pair's improvised slapstick act was an enormous hit that led to a ten-year partnership. Martin went on to become a Vegas fixture and a part of the famed Rat Pack. The singer had the business savvy to control rights to his recordings and performances, which eventually made him a very wealthy man. He appeared in several films, recorded more than six hundred songs and created a hard-drinking, womanizing image that became the centerpiece of his television variety series.

TONY MARTIN
(B. 1913)

Born Alvin Morris in San Francisco, Tony Martin had dreams of becoming an actor. After moving to Hollywood, he appeared frequently on the radio program of George Burns and Gracie Allen. He landed bit parts in several films before he began appearing as himself in a long string of films and television specials and shows. Serving in the military in World War II, he sang with Captain Glenn Miller's band. In addition to maintaining a long career, which found him performing in San Francisco in 2009, at age 95, Martin was married to Cyd Charisse for sixty years — one of Hollywood's longest marriages. Martin's recording of "There's No Tomorrow," based on the Italian song, "O sole mio," spent twenty-seven weeks on the charts, reaching the #2 spot. His recording of "I Get Ideas" hit #3, spending thirty weeks on the charts.

JOHNNY MATHIS
(B. 1935)

Born in Gilmer, Texas, John Royce Mathis spent most of his childhood in San Francisco. Mathis began voice lessons at age thirteen, studying vocal technique, classical music and opera. A strong athlete, he entered college as an English and Physical Education major and was invited to trials for the 1956 Olympic games. But a Columbia Records contract arrived at the same time as the Olympic invitation, changing his path. His 1957 recording of "Chances Are" took him to the top of the charts. His Ed Sullivan show appearance that same year made him a household name in the U.S. In 1958 his *Johnny's Greatest Hits* album hit the *Billboard* Top Albums chart, where it stayed for four hundred and ninety continuous weeks — just short of ten years. It remains one of the most popular albums of all time.

JOHNNY MERCER
(1909-1976)

John Herndon Mercer wrote lyrics to more than 1,000 songs, in musicals, films and popular music. Born into old money in Savannah, Georgia, he is also remembered as a singer, songwriter and co-founder of Capitol Records. Mercer left the South in 1928, when his father's fortune evaporated. After moving to New York City he tried his hand at acting but found work writing lyrics and songs. When a Hollywood job offer came from RKO in 1933, he took it. Over the course of his career, Mercer created hits with such greats as Harold Arlen, Henry Mancini, Harry Warren, Jerome Kern, Marvin Hamlisch and others. Mercer received two "Song of the Year" GRAMMY Awards and four Academy Awards®. He was inducted into the Songwriters Hall of Fame in 1971.

MATT MONRO
(1930-1985)

London-born Terence Edward Parsons sang under the names Terry Fitzgerald and Al Jordan before settling on a stage name. He dropped out of school at age fourteen and worked odd jobs, enlisting in the British Army at seventeen. After twelve years in the service, he returned to London and worked as a bus driver, singing band gigs in his off hours. He did some recording with Decca in those years, recording more than forty commercial jingles in Britain to make ends meet. A Sinatra imitation done for a demo disc, under the name Fred Flange, brought the singer his big break. Before long he had his own television series in Britain and was scoring hits there and in the U.S. He toured the U.S. and appeared on popular American variety shows of the 1960s. Later, Monro released entire albums in Spanish, and enjoyed global fame.

VAUGHN MONROE
(1911-1973)

Born in Akron, Ohio, baritone Vaughn Wilton Monroe's enormous, baritone voice won him nicknames like "old leather tonsils" and "the baritone with muscles" during the big band era. Raised in Wisconsin, Pennsylvania and Massachusetts, he was also a noted trumpeter, trombonist and bandleader, forming a band in Boston in 1940 as lead vocalist. He put a number of hits on the charts in the 1940s, including "There! I've Said It Again," in 1945. In later years, Monroe would say that "Ballerina" was his best recorded performance. As popular taste in music shifted from swing to rock, Monroe tried his hand at singing cowboy films for a time. He worked in television and radio, hosting the *Camel Caravan* for years. An avid pilot, he was known for flying himself to engagements.

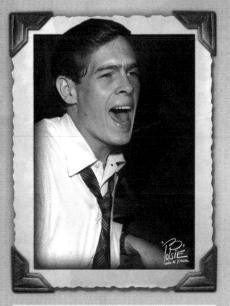

JOHNNIE RAY
(1927-1990)

John Alvin Ray lost most of the hearing in one ear as a child, but still built a singing career that took him around the world. Born in Hopewell, Oregon, the singer, songwriter and pianist was one of the pivotal transition singers between the era of the crooners and era of the rockers. His jazz- and blues-flavored style and on-stage theatrics influenced the likes of Elvis, Jerry Lee Lewis and others. His recording of "Cry" spent eleven weeks at #1 on the charts. Ray made numerous television appearances and performed at the Tropicana in Las Vegas. He developed a huge following in Europe and Australia and was honored with a star on the Hollywood Walk of Fame. Called the most popular singer of the pre-Elvis era, he suffered the effects of a tumultuous personal life.

FRANK SINATRA
(1915-1998)

Whether he was called "Ol' Blue Eyes," "The Chairman of the Board," or "The Voice," Francis Albert Sinatra was undeniably one of the most important entertainers of the 20th century. He dropped out of a New Jersey high school to sing, landing gigs with bands led by Harry James and Tommy Dorsey, striking out on his own in the early 1940s. Sinatra was a heartthrob – women swooned when he sang. He was also a tough character, the rattiest of the "Rat Pack." Men emulated his macho image. Meanwhile, Sinatra sang, acted and built an entertainment empire. He won three Academy Awards®, nine GRAMMY Awards and a Lifetime Achievement GRAMMY. He was an enormous star before rock 'n' roll hit the airwaves in the early 1950s, and put out his best-selling album a half-century later.

MEL TORMÉ
(1925-1999)

Melvin Howard Tormé hated the nickname "The Velvet Fog." Raised in Chicago, Tormé was a child actor in radio days and worked the vaudeville circuit as a child as well. He and Frank Sinatra made their film debuts in *Higher and Higher*, in 1943. Tormé formed a vocal quintet called the Mel-Tones, going solo in 1947 with a crooning, pop style. During the 1950s he brought his laid-back style to several jazz recordings, a dream come true for him, and he continued recording jazz throughout his life. Tormé had his own television show for a short time and appeared in more than twenty films. He also appeared on numerous television shows, including the series *Night Court* and *Seinfeld*. Although Tormé wrote more than three hundred songs and won two GRAMMY Awards, as well as a Lifetime Achievement GRAMMY, he scored only one #1 hit in his long career.

BOBBY VINTON
(B. 1935)

Known by fans as the "Polish Prince," Stanley Robert Vinton, Jr. was born in Canonsburg, Pennsylvania, the son of a local bandleader. Singing in his first band at age sixteen, Vinton earned a degree in composition from Duquesne University, where he learned to play quite a few musical instruments. But he is remembered, according to *Billboard* magazine, as "the all-time most successful love singer of the Rock era." His big break came on Guy Lombardo's *TV Talent Scouts* in 1960. Three years later he took the song "Blue Velvet" to the top of the charts. Although Vinton scored more #1 hits between 1962 and 1972 than any other male solo singer, "Blue Velvet" remains his most famous song. He had his own television variety show for three years and was honored with a star on the Hollywood Walk of Fame.

JOE WILLIAMS
(1918-1999)

Born Joseph Goreed in Cordele, Georgia, baritone jazz singer Joe Williams grew up with his mother, grandmother and aunt in Chicago. He sang in a Gospel quartet, The Jubilee Boys, and with Chicago-area bands in his teens, dropping out of school at sixteen. Although he sang with Jimmy Noone's band, Lionel Hampton's band, and Coleman Hawkins, he first found fame singing with Count Basie's orchestra in 1954. He scored the biggest hit of his career with Basie, "Every Day I Have the Blues," in 1955 and was inducted into the GRAMMY Hall of Fame in 1992 for his recording of the song. In his later years he had a recurring television role as Grandpa Al on *The Cosby Show*. In 1983 he was honored with a star on the Hollywood Walk of Fame and received a GRAMMY in 1984.

AC-CENT-TCHU-ATE THE POSITIVE

from the Motion Picture HERE COME THE WAVES

Lyric by JOHNNY MERCER
Music by HAROLD ARLEN

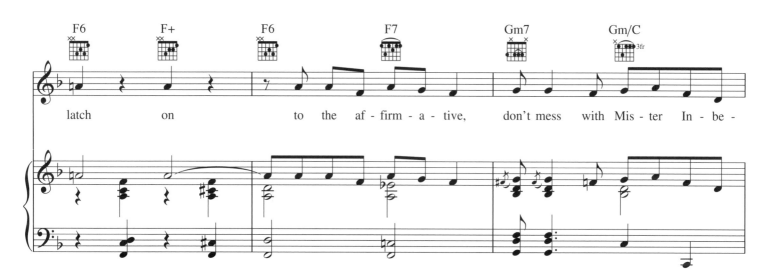

ALRIGHT, OKAY, YOU WIN

Words and Music by SID WYCHE
and MAYME WATTS

BABY
(You've Got What It Takes)

Words and Music by CLYDE OTIS
and MURRAY STEIN

Moderate Shuffle

Well, now it takes more ___ than a rob - in to make the win - ter go; ___ and it takes two lips of fire ___ to melt a - way the snow. ___ Well, it

takes two hearts a-cook - in' to make a fire ___ grow, ___

___ and, ba - by, you've got what it takes. ___

___ You know it takes a lot of

kiss - in' to make a ro - mance sweet. ___ Ooh, ___ it

more than a life-time to prove that I'll be true; —

— but it takes some-bod-y spe-cial to

make me say, "I do," — and, ba-by, you've got what it takes. —

Well, now it

BODY AND SOUL

Words by EDWARD HEYMAN,
ROBERT SOUR and FRANK EYTON
Music by JOHN GREEN

BABY, IT'S COLD OUTSIDE

from the Motion Picture NEPTUNE'S DAUGHTER

By FRANK LOESSER

BALLERINA

Words and Music by BOB RUSSELL
and CARL SIGMAN

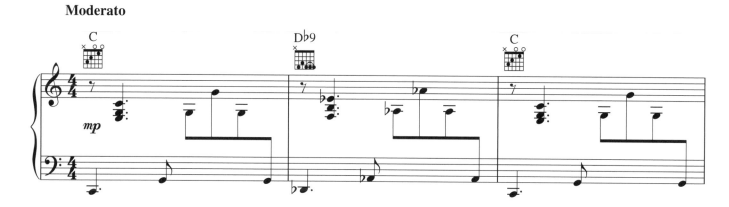

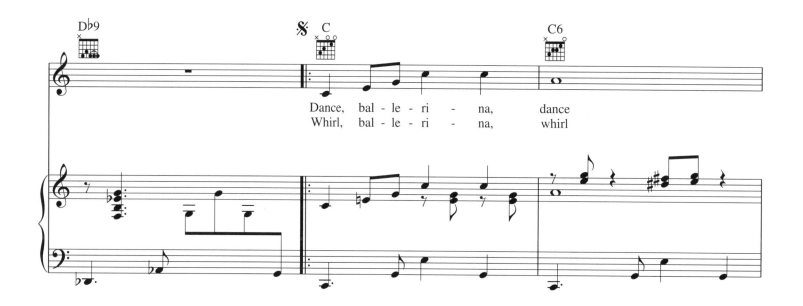

Dance, bal - le - ri - na, dance
Whirl, bal - le - ri - na, whirl

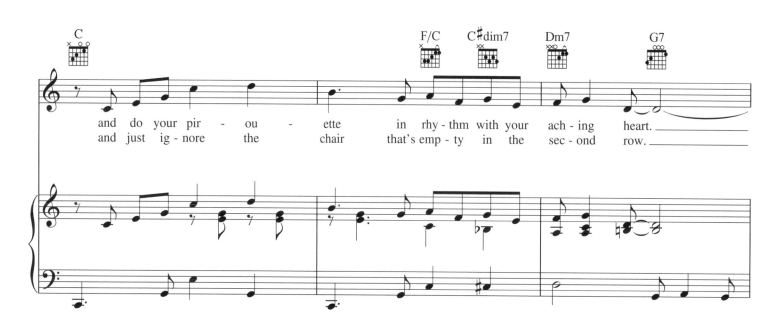

and do your pir - ou - ette in rhy - thm with your ach - ing heart. _____
and just ig - nore the chair that's emp - ty in the sec - ond row. _____

BEWITCHED
from PAL JOEY

Words by LORENZ HART
Music by RICHARD RODGERS

BEYOND THE SEA

By ALBERT LASRY and CHARLES TRENET
English Lyrics by JACK LAWRENCE

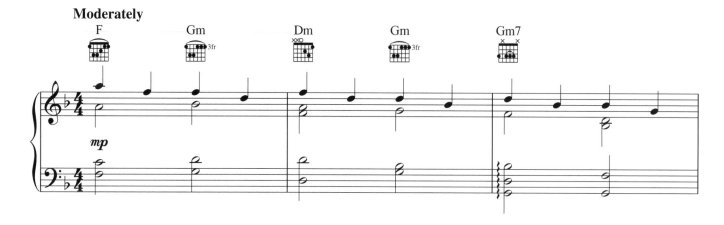

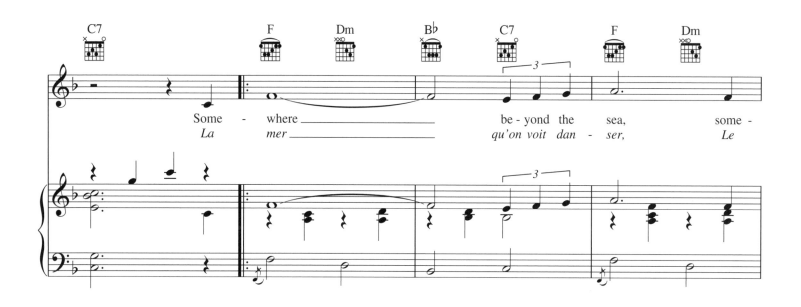

Some - where _____ be - yond the sea, some -
La mer _____ qu'on voit dan - ser, Le

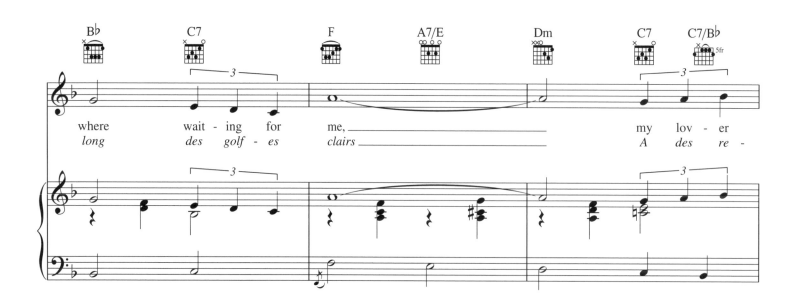

where wait - ing for me, _____ my lov - er
long des golf - es clairs _____ A des re -

50

BLUE VELVET

Words and Music by BERNIE WAYNE
and LEE MORRIS

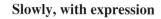

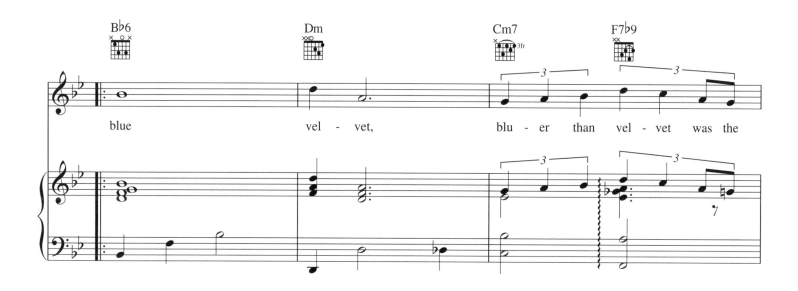

CANDY

Words and Music by MACK DAVID,
ALEX KRAMER and JOAN WHITNEY

CHANCES ARE

Words by AL STILLMAN
Music by ROBERT ALLEN

CARELESS HANDS

Words and Music by CARL SIGMAN
and BOB HILLIARD

CHANGE PARTNERS

from the RKO Radio Motion Picture CAREFREE

Words and Music by
IRVING BERLIN

Ask him to sit this one out, and while you're a- lone ____

____ I'll tell the wait- er to tell him he's

want- ed on the tel - e - phone. You've been locked ____

in his arms ____

CHEEK TO CHEEK
from the RKO Radio Motion Picture TOP HAT

Words and Music by
IRVING BERLIN

72

THE CHRISTMAS SONG
(Chestnuts Roasting on an Open Fire)

Music and Lyric by MEL TORMÉ
and ROBERT WELLS

moth-er's child ___ is gon-na spy ___ to see if rein-deer ___ real-ly know how to

fly. And so I'm of-fer-ing this sim-ple phrase to

kids from one to nine-ty-two. Al-though it's been said man-y

times, man-y ways, "Mer-ry Christ-mas to you." you."

COLD, COLD HEART

Words and Music by
HANK WILLIAMS

COME RAIN OR COME SHINE

from ST. LOUIS WOMAN

Words by JOHNNY MERCER
Music by HAROLD ARLEN

82

CRY

Words and Music by
CHURCHILL KOHLMAN

A COTTAGE FOR SALE

Words by LARRY CONLEY
Music by WILLARD ROBISON

Our lit-tle dream cas-tle with ev-'ry dream gone, ____ is lone-ly and si-lent, the

DEAR HEARTS AND GENTLE PEOPLE

Words by BOB HILLIARD
Music by SAMMY FAIN

There's a place I'd like to be and it's back in Ten-nes-see, where your friend-ly neigh-bors smile and say hel-lo. It's a

DIDN'T WE

Words and Music by
JIMMY WEBB

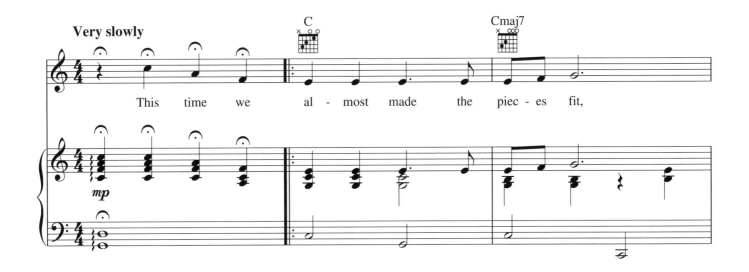

This time we al-most made the piec-es fit,

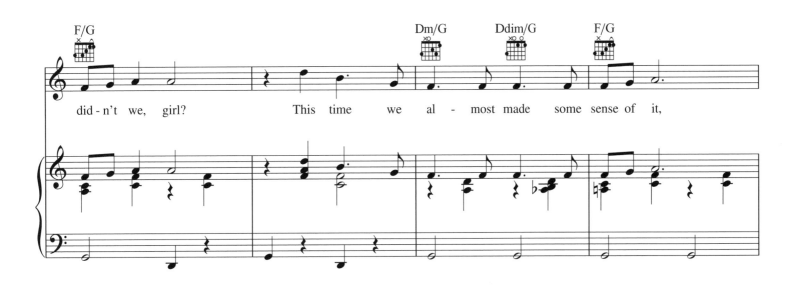

did-n't we, girl? This time we al-most made some sense of it,

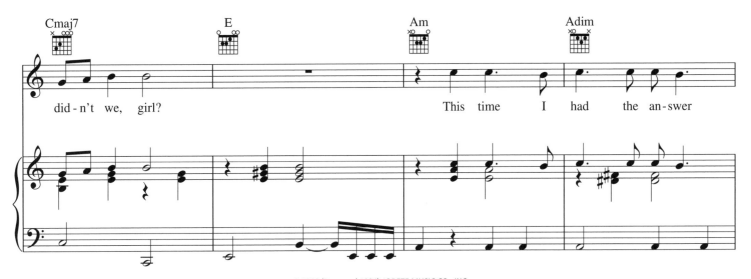

did-n't we, girl? This time I had the an-swer

DO I LOVE YOU BECAUSE YOU'RE BEAUTIFUL?

from CINDERELLA

Lyrics by OSCAR HAMMERSTEIN II
Music by RICHARD RODGERS

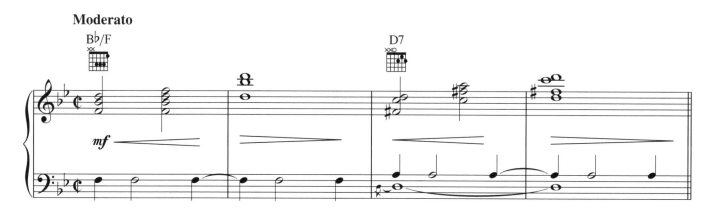

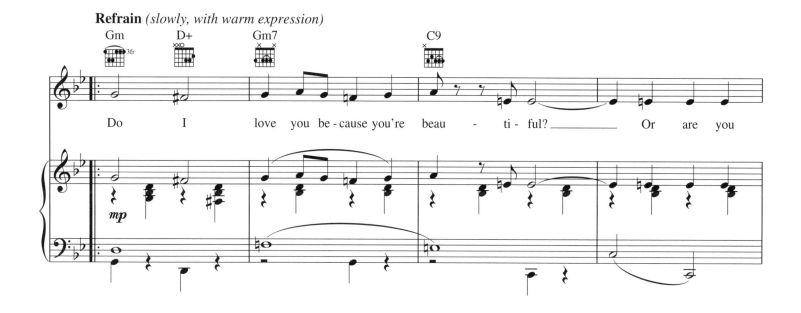

Do I love you be-cause you're beau-ti-ful? _____ Or are you

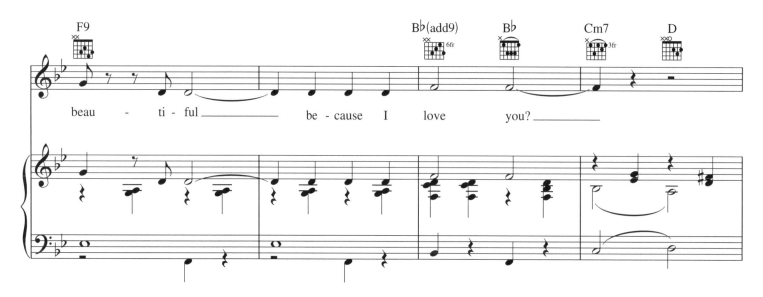

beau-ti-ful _____ be-cause I love you? _____

DON'T LET THE STARS GET IN YOUR EYES

Words and Music by
SLIM WILLET

DREAM LOVER

Words and Music by
BOBBY DARIN

EVERYDAY I HAVE THE BLUES

Words and Music by
PETER CHATMAN

(I Love You)
FOR SENTIMENTAL REASONS

Words by DEEK WATSON
Music by WILLIAM BEST

FRIENDLY PERSUASION
from the Motion Picture FRIENDLY PERSUASION

Words by PAUL FRANCIS WEBSTER
Music by DIMITRI TIOMKIN

HOW DEEP IS THE OCEAN
(How High Is the Sky)

Words and Music by
IRVING BERLIN

How much do I love you? I'll tell you no lie, how deep is the o - cean, how high is the sky? How man - y

GEORGIA ON MY MIND

Words by STUART GORRELL
Music by HOAGY CARMICHAEL

GONNA BUILD A MOUNTAIN

from the Musical Production STOP THE WORLD – I WANT TO GET OFF

Words and Music by LESLIE BRICUSSE
and ANTHONY NEWLEY

Grandioso

grace. With a fine young son

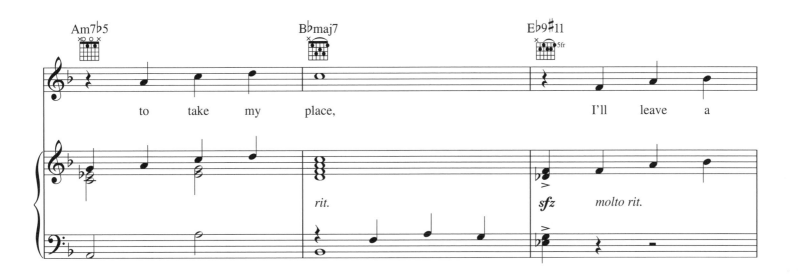

to take my place, I'll leave a

son in my heav-en on earth with the good Lord's grace.

Extra Verses

Gonna build a heaven from a little hell.
Gonna build a heaven, and I know darn well,
With a fine young son to take my place
There'll be a sun in my heaven on earth
With the good Lord's grace.

Gonna build a mountain from a little hill.
Gonna build a mountain – least I hope I will.
Gonna build a mountain – gonna build it high.
I don't know how I'm gonna do it –
Only know I'm gonna try.

I ALMOST LOST MY MIND

Words and Music by
IVORY JOE HUNTER

I BELIEVE

Words and Music by ERVIN DRAKE, IRVIN GRAHAM,
JIMMY SHIRL and AL STILLMAN

I GET IDEAS

Words by DORCAS COCHRAN
Music by JULIO C. SANDERS

When we are danc-ing and you're dan-ger-ous-ly near me, I get i-deas,____ I get i-deas.____ I wan-na hold you so much clos-er than I dare to, I wan-na

I'M WALKING BEHIND YOU
(Look over Your Shoulder)

Words and Music by
BILLY REID

I'VE GOT THE WORLD ON A STRING

Lyric by TED KOEHLER
Music by HAROLD ARLEN

Mer - ry month of May,   sun - ny

I'VE GOT YOU UNDER MY SKIN

from BORN TO DANCE

Words and Music by
COLE PORTER

IF

Words by ROBERT HARGREAVES
and STANLEY J. DAMERELL
Music by TOLCHARD EVANS

153

IT'S JUST A MATTER OF TIME

Words and Music by BROOK BENTON, CLYDE OTIS
and BELFORD HENDRICKS

THE IMPOSSIBLE DREAM
(The Quest)
from MAN OF LA MANCHA

Lyric by JOE DARION
Music by MITCH LEIGH

IT'S NOT FOR ME TO SAY

Words by AL STILLMAN
Music by ROBERT ALLEN

JUST IN TIME
from BELLS ARE RINGING

Words by BETTY COMDEN and ADOLPH GREEN
Music by JULE STYNE

JUST WALKING IN THE RAIN

Words and Music by JOHNNY BRAGG
and ROBERT S. RILEY

Just walk-ing in the rain, _____ get-ting soak-ing wet; _____ tor-tur-ing my heart _____ by try-ing to for-get. _____ Just walk-ing in the

LAZY RIVER

from THE BEST YEARS OF OUR LIVES

Words and Music by HOAGY CARMICHAEL
and SIDNEY ARODIN

172

LEARNIN' THE BLUES

Words and Music by
DOLORES "VICKI" SILVERS

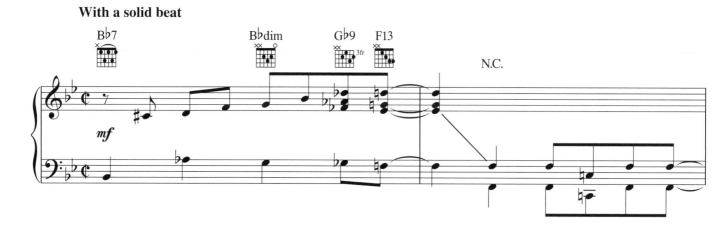

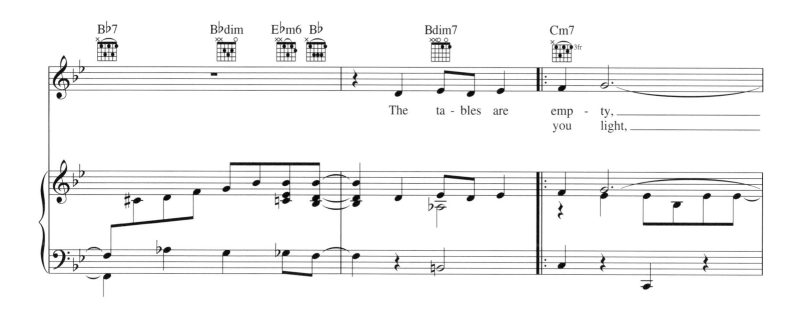

The ta-bles are emp-ty, _____
you light, _____

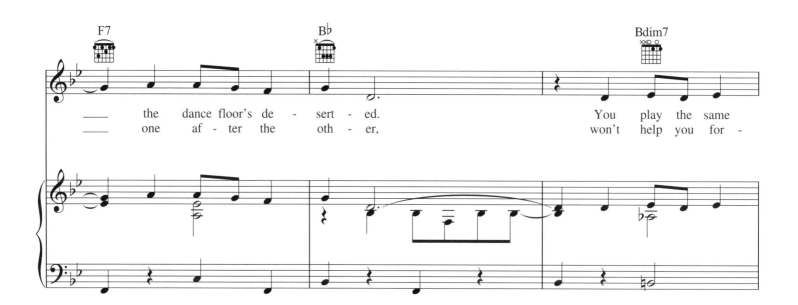

_____ the dance floor's de-sert-ed.
_____ one af-ter the oth-er,

You play the same
won't help you for-

LOLLIPOPS AND ROSES

Words and Music by
TONY VELONA

LOVE LETTERS IN THE SAND

Words by NICK KENNY and CHARLES KENNY
Music by J. FRED COOTS

MR. LONELY

Words and Music by BOBBY VINTON
and GENE ALLAN

MISTY

Words by JOHNNY BURKE
Music by ERROLL GARNER

Slowly, with expression

Look at me, I'm as help-less as a kit-ten up a tree and I feel like I'm cling-ing to a cloud, I can't ___ un-der-stand, ___ I get mist-y just hold-ing your hand. _____ Walk my way and a

MONA LISA

from the Paramount Picture CAPTAIN CAREY, U.S.A.

Words and Music by JAY LIVINGSTON
and RAY EVANS

MOONLIGHT GAMBLER

Words by BOB HILLIARD
Music by PHILIP SPRINGER

Slow, ambling rhythm

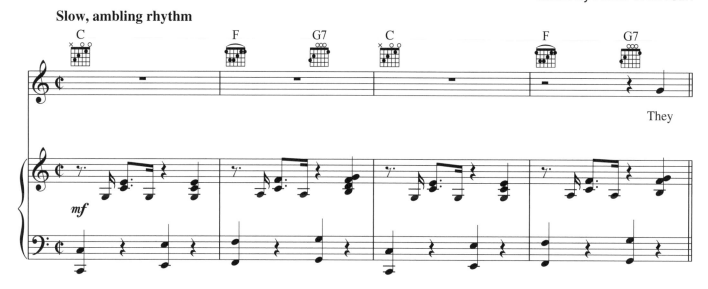

They

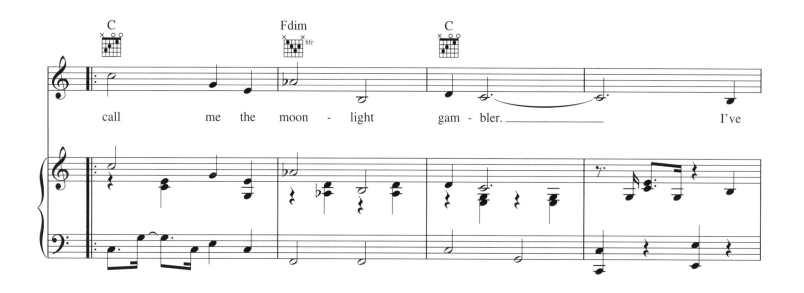

call me the moon - light gam - bler. _____ I've

gam - bled for love and lost. _____ When I

MY FOOLISH HEART

from MY FOOLISH HEART

Words by NED WASHINGTON
Music by VICTOR YOUNG

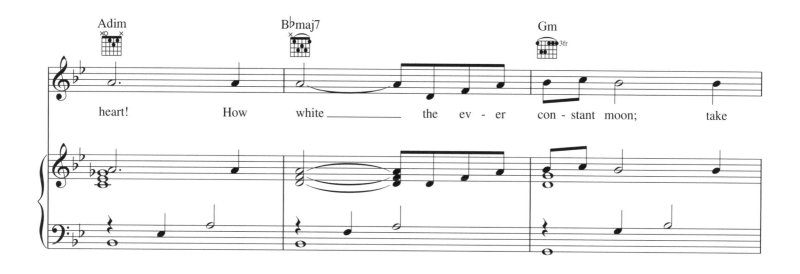

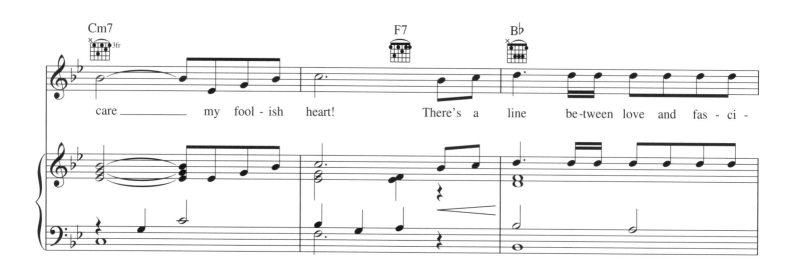

MY ONE AND ONLY LOVE

Words by ROBERT MELLIN
Music by GUY WOOD

MY KIND OF GIRL

Words and Music by
LESLIE BRICUSSE

NATURE BOY

Words and Music by
EDEN AHBEZ

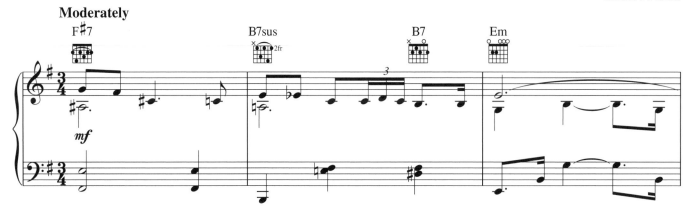

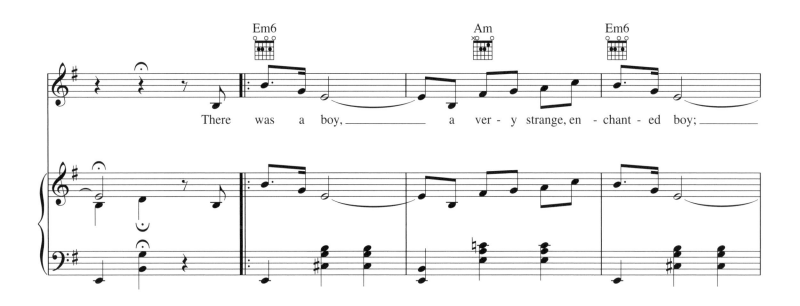

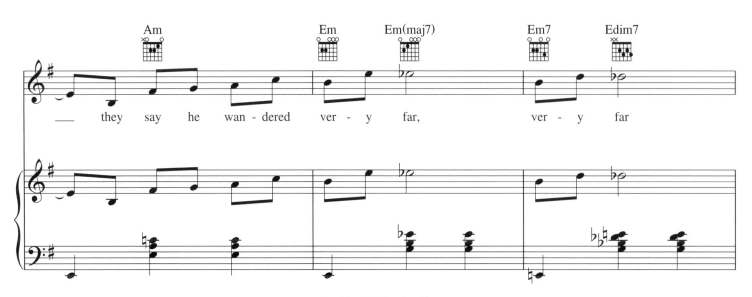

THE NEARNESS OF YOU

from the Paramount Picture ROMANCE IN THE DARK

Words by NED WASHINGTON
Music by HOAGY CARMICHAEL

NIGHT SONG
from GOLDEN BOY

Lyric by LEE ADAMS
Music by CHARLES STROUSE

OH! WHAT IT SEEMED TO BE

Words and Music by BENNIE BENJAMIN,
GEORGE DAVID WEISS and FRANKIE CARLE

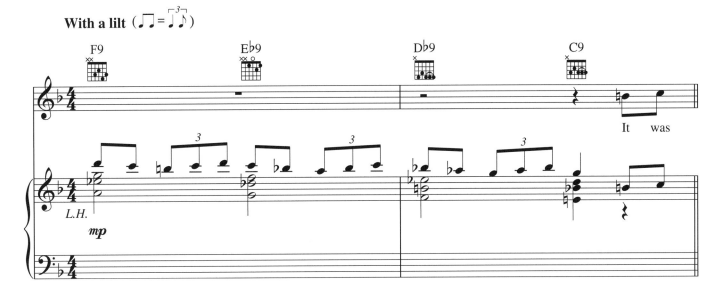

OH! MY PA-PA
(O Mein Papa)

English Words by JOHN TURNER and GEOFFREY PARSONS
Music and Original Lyric by PAUL BURKHARD

OLE BUTTERMILK SKY

from the Motion Picture CANYON PASSAGE

Words and Music by HOAGY CARMICHAEL
and JACK BROOKS

229

ON THE STREET WHERE YOU LIVE

from MY FAIR LADY

Words by ALAN JAY LERNER
Music by FREDERICK LOEWE

A RAINY NIGHT IN GEORGIA

Words and Music by
TONY JOE WHITE

1. Hov- erin' by my suit- case, tryin' to find a warm place to
2. Ne- on signs a-flash- in', tax- i- cabs and bus- es pass- in'
3. *(See additional lyrics)*

spend the night; a heav- y rain a-fall- in';
through the night; the dis- tant moan- in' of a train

seems I hear your voice call- in', "It's all right."
seems to play a sad re- frain to the night:

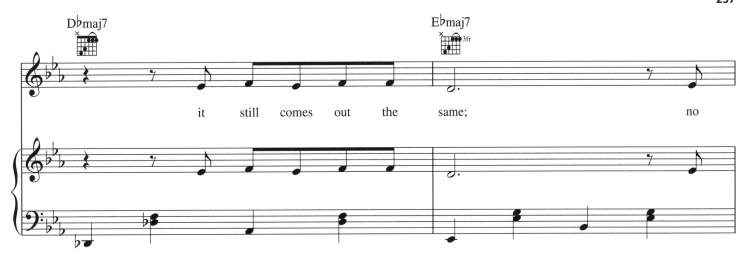

it still comes out the same;   no

mat- ter how you look at it, think of it, you

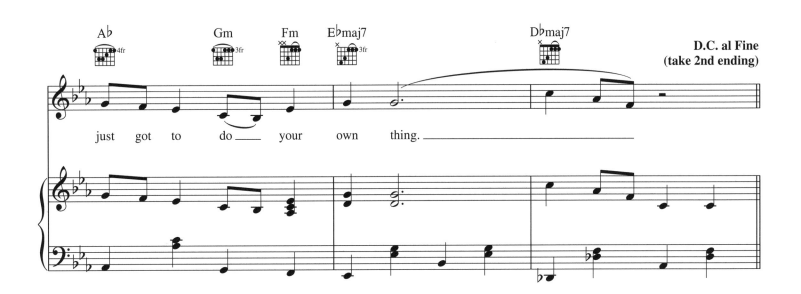

just got to do ___ your own thing. ___

D.C. al Fine
(take 2nd ending)

Additional Lyrics

3. I find me a place in a box car,
   So I take out my guitar to pass some time;
   Late at night when it's hard to rest,
   I hold your picture to my chest, and I'm all right.
   Chorus

PISTOL PACKIN' MAMA

Words and Music by
AL DEXTER

Moderate Blues tempo

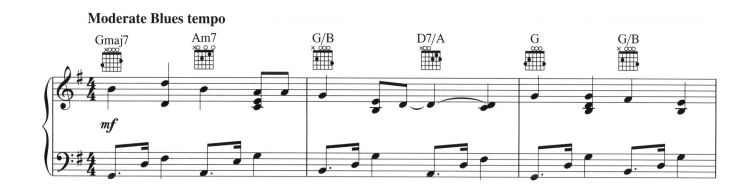

Drink - in' beer in a cab - a - ret, ___ and
She kicked out my ___ wind - shield, ___ she
Drink - in' beer in a cab - a - ret, ___ and

was I hav - in' fun! Un - til one night she
hit me o - ver the head, she cussed and cried she and
danc - ing with a blonde, un - til one night she

RED ROSES FOR A BLUE LADY

Words and Music by SID TEPPER
and ROY C. BENNETT

RETURN TO ME

Words and Music by DANNY DI MINNO
and CARMEN LOMBARDO

244

ROCKIN' CHAIR

Words and Music by
HOAGY CARMICHAEL

248

SHE LOVES ME
from SHE LOVES ME

Words by SHELDON HARNICK
Music by JERRY BOCK

SEEMS LIKE OLD TIMES

Lyric and Music by JOHN JACOB LOEB
and CARMEN LOMBARDO

STRANGER IN PARADISE
from KISMET

Words and Music by ROBERT WRIGHT
and GEORGE FORREST
(Music based on Themes of A. BORODIN)

SWAY
(Quien Será)

English Words by NORMAN GIMBEL
Spanish Words and Music by PABLO BELTRAN RUIZ

When ma-rim-ba rhy-thms start to play, dance with me,
Quien se-rá la que me quie-ra a mí *Quien se-rá*

make me sway.___ Like the la-zy o-cean hugs the shore,
Quien se-rá___ *Quien se-rá la que me dé su a-mor*

hold me close, sway me more._____ Like a flow-er bend-ing
Quien se-rá *Quien se-rá_____* *Yo no sé si la po-*

TEACH ME TONIGHT

Words by SAMMY CAHN
Music by GENE DePAUL

THAT'S MY DESIRE

Words by CARROLL LOVEDAY
Music by HELMY KRESA

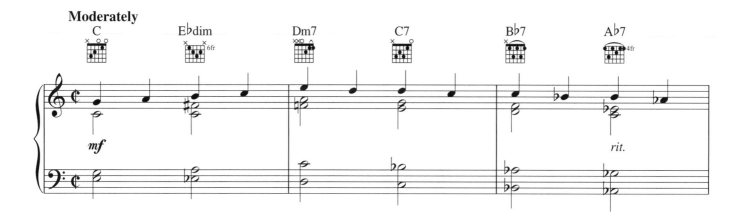

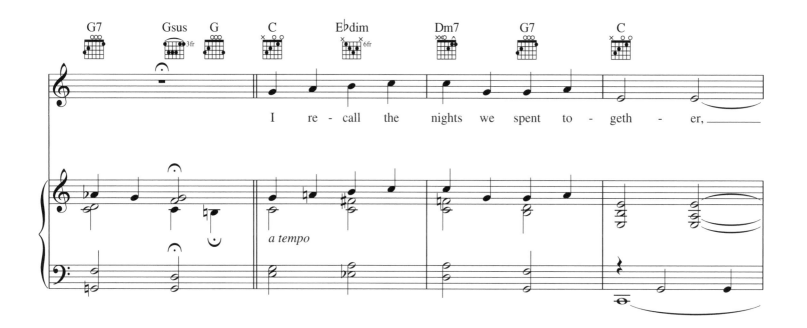

I re-call the nights we spent to-geth - er, _____

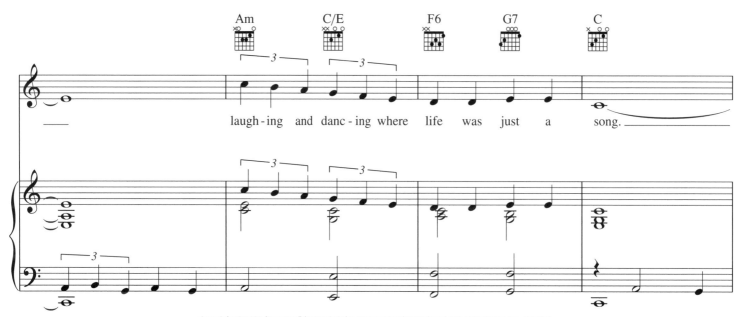

_____ laugh-ing and danc-ing where life was just a song. _____

THERE! I'VE SAID IT AGAIN

Words and Music by DAVE MANN
and REDD EVANS

THERE'S NO TOMORROW

Written by AL HOFFMAN,
LEO CORDAY and LEON CARR

THERE IS NO GREATER LOVE

Words by MARTY SYMES
Music by ISHAM JONES

THEY SAY IT'S WONDERFUL
from the Stage Production ANNIE GET YOUR GUN

Words and Music by
IRVING BERLIN

Slowly

Annie: Ru - mors fly and you
Frank: Ru - mors fly and you

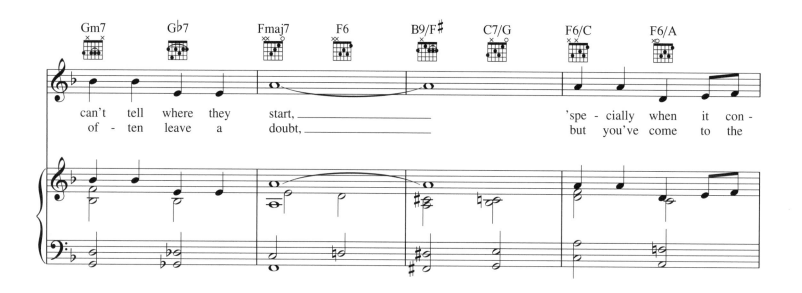

can't tell where they start, _____ 'spe - cially when it con -
of - ten leave a doubt, _____ but you've come to the

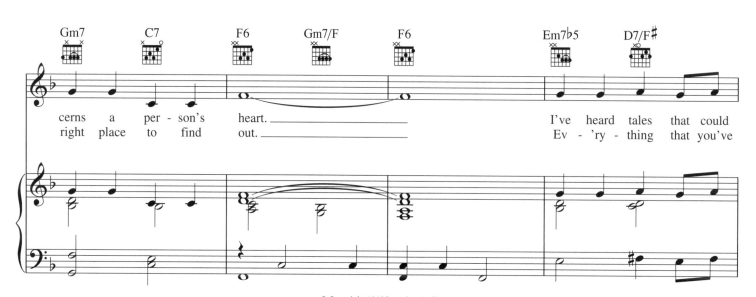

cerns a per - son's heart. _____ I've heard tales that could
right place to find out. _____ Ev - 'ry - thing that you've

TILL THE END OF TIME

from TILL THE END OF TIME

(Based on Chopin's Polonaise)
Words and Music by BUDDY KAYE
and TED MOSSMAN

WALKIN' MY BABY BACK HOME

Words and Music by ROY TURK
and FRED E. AHLERT

The Way You Look Tonight

from SWING TIME

Words by DOROTHY FIELDS
Music by JEROME KERN

296

WHAT KIND OF FOOL AM I?

from the Musical Production STOP THE WORLD – I WANT TO GET OFF

Words and Music by LESLIE BRICUSSE
and ANTHONY NEWLEY

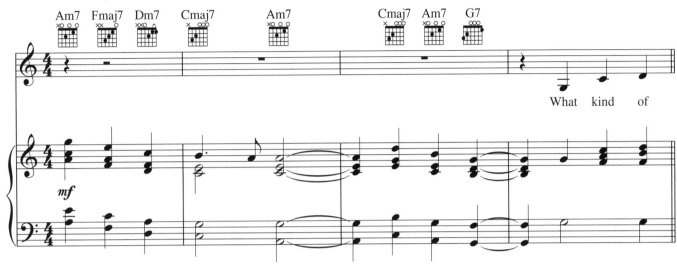

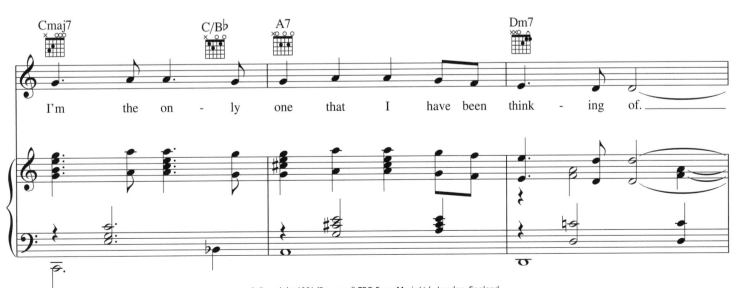

WHEN I FALL IN LOVE

from ONE MINUTE TO ZERO

Words by EDWARD HEYMAN
Music by VICTOR YOUNG

YOU'RE BREAKING MY HEART

Words and Music by PAT GENARO
and SUNNY SKYLAR

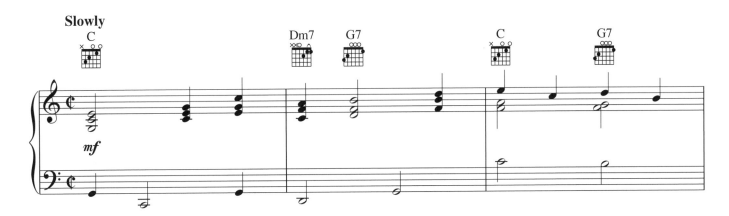

You're break - ing my heart 'cause you're leav - ing. ___ You've

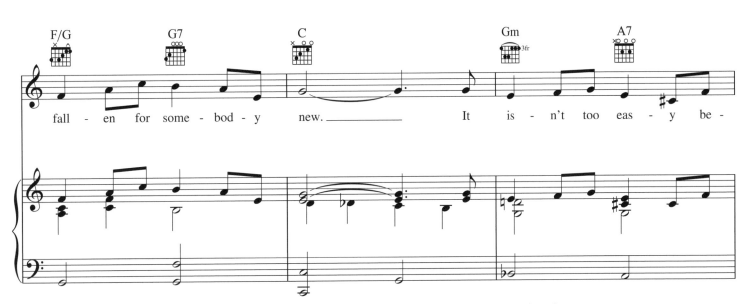

fall - en for some - bod - y new. ___ It is - n't too eas - y be -

WISH YOU WERE HERE

from WISH YOU WERE HERE

Words and Music by
HAROLD ROME

YOU'RE NOBODY 'TIL SOMEBODY LOVES YOU

Words and Music by RUSS MORGAN,
LARRY STOCK and JAMES CAVANAUGH

ZIP-A-DEE-DOO-DAH
from Walt Disney's SONG OF THE SOUTH

Words by RAY GILBERT
Music by ALLIE WRUBEL

Classic Collections Of Your Favorite Songs

arranged for piano, voice, and guitar.

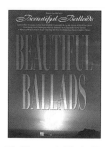

Beautiful Ballads
A massive collection of 87 songs, including: April in Paris • Autumn in New York • Call Me Irresponsible • Cry Me a River • I Wish You Love • I'll Be Seeing You • If • Imagine • Isn't It Romantic? • It's Impossible (Somos Novios) • Mona Lisa • Moon River • People • The Way We Were • A Whole New World (Aladdin's Theme) • and more.
00311679 ....$17.95

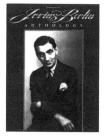

Irving Berlin Anthology
A comprehensive collection of 61 timeless songs with a bio, song background notes, and photos. Songs include: Always • Blue Skies • Cheek to Cheek • God Bless America • Marie • Puttin' on the Ritz • Steppin' Out with My Baby • There's No Business Like Show Business • White Christmas • (I Wonder Why?) You're Just in Love • and more.
00312493 ....$22.95

The Big Book of Standards
86 classics essential to any music library, including: April in Paris • Autumn in New York • Blue Skies • Cheek to Cheek • Heart and Soul • I Left My Heart in San Francisco • In the Mood • Isn't It Romantic? • Mona Lisa • Moon River • The Nearness of You • Out of Nowhere • Spanish Eyes • Star Dust • Stella by Starlight • That Old Black Magic • They Say It's Wonderful • What Now My Love • and more.
00311667 ....$19.95

Broadway Deluxe
This exciting collection of 125 of Broadway's biggest show tunes is deluxe indeed! Includes such showstoppers as: Bewitched • Cabaret • Camelot • Day by Day • Hello Young Lovers • I Could Have Danced All Night • I've Grown Accustomed to Her Face • If Ever I Would Leave You • The Lady Is a Tramp • I Talk to the Trees • My Heart Belongs to Daddy • Oklahoma • September Song • Seventy Six Trombones • Try to Remember • and more!
00309245 ....$24.95

The Great American Songbook – The Singers
Crooners, wailers, shouters, balladeers: some of our greatest pop vocalists have poured their hearts and souls into the musical gems of the Great American Songbook. This folio features 100 of these classics by Louis Armstrong, Tony Bennett, Rosemary Clooney, Nat "King" Cole, Bing Crosby, Doris Day, Ella Fitzgerald, Judy Garland, Dean Martin, Frank Sinatra, Barbra Streisand, Mel Tormé, and others.
00311433 ....$24.95

I'll Be Seeing You: 50 Songs of World War II
A salute to the music and memories of WWII, including a year-by-year chronology of events on the homefront, dozens of photos, and 50 radio favorites of the GIs and their families back home, including: Boogie Woogie Bugle Boy • Don't Sit Under the Apple Tree (With Anyone Else But Me) • I Don't Want to Walk Without You • I'll Be Seeing You • Moonlight in Vermont • There's a Star-Spangled Banner Waving Somewhere • You'd Be So Nice to Come Home To • and more.
00311698 ....$19.95

Lounge Music – 2nd Edition
Features over 50 top requests of the martini crowd: All the Way • Fever • I Write the Songs • Misty • Moon River • That's Amore (That's Love) • Yesterday • more.
00310193 ....$15.95

Best of Cole Porter
38 of his classics, including: All of You • Anything Goes • Be a Clown • Don't Fence Me In • I Get a Kick Out of You • In the Still of the Night • Let's Do It (Let's Fall in Love) • Night and Day • You Do Something to Me • and many more.
00311577 ....$14.95

Big Band Favorites
A great collection of 70 of the best Swing Era songs, including: East of the Sun • Honeysuckle Rose • I Can't Get Started with You • I'll Be Seeing You • In the Mood • Let's Get Away from It All • Moonglow • Moonlight in Vermont • Opus One • Stompin' at the Savoy • Tuxedo Junction • more!
00310445 ....$16.95

The Best of Rodgers & Hammerstein
A capsule of 26 classics from this legendary duo. Songs include: Climb Ev'ry Mountain • Edelweiss • Getting to Know You • I'm Gonna Wash That Man Right Outta My Hair • My Favorite Things • Oklahoma • The Surrey with the Fringe on Top • You'll Never Walk Alone • and more.
00308210 ....$16.95

The Best Songs Ever – 5th Edition
Over 70 must-own classics, including: All I Ask of You • Body and Soul • Crazy • Fly Me to the Moon • Here's That Rainy Day • Imagine • Love Me Tender • Memory • Moonlight in Vermont • My Funny Valentine • People • Satin Doll • Save the Best for Last • Tears in Heaven • A Time for Us • The Way We Were • What a Wonderful World • When I Fall in Love • and more.
00359224 .... $22.95

Torch Songs
Sing your heart out with this collection of 59 sultry jazz and big band melancholy masterpieces, including: Angel Eyes • Cry Me a River • I Can't Get Started • I Got It Bad and That Ain't Good • I'm Glad There Is You • Lover Man (Oh, Where Can You Be?) • Misty • My Funny Valentine • Stormy Weather • and many more! 224 pages.
00490446 ....$17.95

THE ULTIMATE SERIES

This comprehensive series features jumbo collections of piano/vocal arrangements with guitar chords. Each volume features an outstanding selection of your favorite songs. Collect them all for the ultimate music library!

Blues
90 blues classics, including: Boom Boom • Born Under a Bad Sign • Gee Baby, Ain't I Good to You • I Can't Quit You Baby • Pride and Joy • (They Call It) Stormy Monday • Sweet Home Chicago • Why I Sing the Blues • and more.
00310723 . . . . $19.95

Broadway Gold
100 show tunes: Beauty and the Beast • Do-Re-Mi • I Whistle a Happy Tune • The Lady Is a Tramp • Memory • My Funny Valentine • Oklahoma • Some Enchanted Evening • Summer Nights • Tomorrow • many more.
00361396 . . . . $21.95

Broadway Platinum
100 popular Broadway show tunes, featuring: Consider Yourself • Getting to Know You • Gigi • Do You Hear the People Sing • I'll Be Seeing You • My Favorite Things • People • She Loves Me • Try to Remember • Younger Than Springtime • many more.
00311496 . . . . $22.95

Children's Songbook
66 fun songs for kids: Alphabet Song • Be Our Guest • Bingo • The Brady Bunch • Do-Re-Mi • Hakuna Matata • It's a Small World • Kum Ba Yah • Sesame Street Theme • Tomorrow • Won't You Be My Neighbor? • and more.
00310690 . . . . $18.95

Christmas – Third Edition
Includes: Carol of the Bells • Deck the Hall • Frosty the Snow Man • Gesu Bambino • Good King Wenceslas • Jingle-Bell Rock • Joy to the World • Nuttin' for Christmas • O Holy Night • Rudolph the Red-Nosed Reindeer • Silent Night • What Child Is This? • and more.
00361399 . . . . $19.95

Classic Rock
70 rock classics in one great collection! Includes: Angie • Best of My Love • California Girls • Crazy Little Thing Called Love • Joy to the World • Landslide • Light My Fire • Livin' on a Prayer • (She's) Some Kind of Wonderful • Sultans of Swing • Sweet Emotion • and more.
00310962 . . . . $22.95

Classical Collection
Delightful piano solo arrangements, including: Air on the G String (Bach) • Für Elise (Beethoven) • Seguidilla from *Carmen* (Bizet) • Lullaby (Brahms) • Clair De Lune (Debussy) • The Swan (Saint-Saëns) • Ave Maria (Schubert) • Swan Lake (Tchaikovsky) • dozens more.
00311109 . . . . $17.95

Contemporary Christian
Includes over 40 favorites: Awesome God • Can't Live a Day • El Shaddai • Friends • God Is in Control • His Strength Is Perfect • I Can Only Imagine • One of These Days • Place in This World • and more.
00311224 . . . . $19.95

Country – Second Edition
90 of your favorite country hits: Boot Scootin' Boogie • Chattahoochie • Could I Have This Dance • Crazy • Down at the Twist And Shout • Hey, Good Lookin' • Lucille • When She Cries • and more.
00310036 . . . . $19.95

Gospel
Includes: El Shaddai • His Eye Is on the Sparrow • How Great Thou Art • Just a Closer Walk With Thee • Lead Me, Guide Me • (There'll Be) Peace in the Valley (For Me) • Precious Lord, Take My Hand • Wings of a Dove • and more.
00241009 . . . . $19.95

Jazz Standards
Over 100 great jazz favorites: Ain't Misbehavin' • All of Me • Come Rain or Come Shine • Here's That Rainy Day • I'll Take Romance • Imagination • Li'l Darlin' • Manhattan • Moonglow • Moonlight in Vermont • A Night in Tunisia • The Party's Over • Solitude • Star Dust • and more.
00361407 . . . . $19.95

Latin Songs
80 hot Latin favorites, including: Amapola (Pretty Little Poppy) • Amor • Bésame Mucho (Kiss Me Much) • Blame It on the Bossa Nova • Feelings (¿Dime?) • Malagueña • Mambo No. 5 • Perfidia • Slightly out of Tune (Desafinado) • What a Diff'rence a Day Made • and more.
00310689 . . . . $19.95

Love and Wedding Songbook
90 songs of devotion including: The Anniversary Waltz • Canon in D • Endless Love • Forever and Ever, Amen • Just the Way You Are • Love Me Tender • Sunrise, Sunset • Through the Years • Trumpet Voluntary • and more.
00361445 . . . . $19.95

Movie Music – Second Edition
73 favorites from the big screen, including: Can You Feel the Love Tonight • Chariots of Fire • Cruella De Vil • Driving Miss Daisy • Easter Parade • Forrest Gump • Moon River • That Thing You Do! • Viva Las Vegas • The Way We Were • When I Fall in Love • and more.
00310240 . . . . $19.95

New Age
Includes: Cast Your Fate to the Wind • Chariots of Fire • Cristofori's Dream • A Day Without Rain • The Memory of Trees • The Steamroller • and more.
00311160 . . . . $17.95

Nostalgia Songs
100 great favorites from yesteryear, such as: Ain't We Got Fun? • Alexander's Ragtime Band • Casey Jones • Chicago • Danny Boy • Second Hand Rose • Swanee • Toot, Toot, Tootsie! • 'Way Down Yonder in New Orleans • The Yellow Rose of Texas • You Made Me Love You • and more.
00310730 . . . . $17.95

Pop/Rock
70 of the most popular pop/rock hits of our time, including: Bad, Bad Leroy Brown • Bohemian Rhapsody • Dust in the Wind • Imagine • Invisible Touch • More Than Words • Smooth • Tears in Heaven • Thriller • Walking in Memphis • You Are So Beautiful • and more.
00310963 . . . . $22.95

Reggae
42 favorite reggae hits, including: Get Up Stand Up • I Need a Roof • Jamaica Nice • Legalize It • Miss Jamaica • Rivers of Babylon • Tomorrow People • Uptown Top Ranking • Train to Skaville • Try Jah Love • and more.
00311029 . . . . $18.95

Rock 'N' Roll
100 classics, including: All Shook Up • Bye Bye Love • Duke of Earl • Gloria • Hello Mary Lou • It's My Party • Johnny B. Goode • The Loco-Motion • Lollipop • Surfin' U.S.A. • The Twist • Wooly Bully • Yakety Yak • and more.
00361411 . . . . $21.95

Singalong!
100 of the best-loved popular songs ever: Beer Barrel Polka • Crying in the Chapel • Edelweiss • Feelings • Five Foot Two, Eyes of Blue • For Me and My Gal • Indiana • It's a Small World • Que Sera, Sera • This Land Is Your Land • When Irish Eyes Are Smiling • and more.
00361418 . . . . $18.95

Standard Ballads
91 mellow masterpieces, including: Angel Eyes • Body and Soul • Darn That Dream • Day By Day • Easy to Love • Mona Lisa • Moon River • My Funny Valentine • Smoke Gets in Your Eyes • When I Fall in Love • and more.
00310246 . . . . $19.99

Swing Standards
87 songs to get you swinging, including: Bandstand Boogie • Boogie Woogie Bugle Boy • Heart and Soul • How High the Moon • In the Mood • Moonglow • Satin Doll • Sentimental Journey • Witchcraft • and more.
00310245 . . . . $19.95

TV Themes
More than 90 themes from your favorite TV shows, including: The Addams Family Theme • Cleveland Rocks • Theme from Frasier • Happy Days • Love Boat Theme • Hey, Hey We're the Monkees • Nadia's Theme • Sesame Street Theme • Theme from Star Trek® • and more.
00310841 . . . . $19.95

Prices, contents, and availability subject to change without notice. Availability and pricing may vary outside the U.S.A.

FOR MORE INFORMATION, SEE YOUR LOCAL MUSIC DEALER, OR WRITE TO:

HAL•LEONARD® CORPORATION
7777 W. BLUEMOUND RD. P.O. BOX 13819 MILWAUKEE, WI 53213

www.halleonard.com

0609

Big Books of Music

Our "Big Books" feature big selections of popular titles under one cover, perfect for performing musicians, music aficionados or the serious hobbyist. All books are arranged for piano, voice, and guitar, and feature stay-open binding, so the books lie flat without breaking the spine.

BIG BOOK OF BALLADS
62 songs.
00310485 ....$19.95

BIG BOOK OF BIG BAND HITS
84 songs.
00310701 ....$19.95

BIG BOOK OF BLUEGRASS SONGS
70 songs.
00311484 ....$19.95

BIG BOOK OF BLUES
80 songs.
00311843 ....$19.99

BIG BOOK OF BROADWAY
70 songs.
00311658 ....$19.95

BIG BOOK OF CHILDREN'S SONGS
55 songs.
00359261 ....$14.95

GREAT BIG BOOK OF CHILDREN'S SONGS
76 songs.
00310002 ....$14.95

FANTASTIC BIG BOOK OF CHILDREN'S SONGS
66 songs.
00311062 ....$17.95

MIGHTY BIG BOOK OF CHILDREN'S SONGS
65 songs.
00310467 ....$14.95

REALLY BIG BOOK OF CHILDREN'S SONGS
63 songs.
00310372 ....$16.95

BIG BOOK OF CHILDREN'S MOVIE SONGS
66 songs.
00310731 ....$19.95

BIG BOOK OF CHRISTMAS SONGS
126 songs.
00311520 ....$19.95

BIG BOOK OF CLASSIC ROCK
77 songs.
00310801 ....$22.95

BIG BOOK OF CLASSICAL MUSIC
100 songs.
00310508 ....$19.95

BIG BOOK OF CONTEMPORARY CHRISTIAN FAVORITES
50 songs.
00310021 ....$19.95

BIG BOOK OF COUNTRY MUSIC
63 songs.
00310188 ....$19.95

BIG BOOK OF COUNTRY ROCK
64 songs.
00311748 ....$19.99

BIG BOOK OF DISCO & FUNK
70 songs.
00310878 ....$19.95

BIG BOOK OF EARLY ROCK N' ROLL
99 songs.
00310398 ....$19.95

BIG BOOK OF '50S & '60S SWINGING SONGS
67 songs.
00310982 ....$19.95

BIG BOOK OF FOLK POP ROCK
79 songs.
00311125 ....$24.95

BIG BOOK OF FRENCH SONGS
70 songs.
00311154 ....$19.95

BIG BOOK OF GOSPEL SONGS
100 songs.
00310604 ....$19.95

BIG BOOK OF HYMNS
125 hymns.
00310510 ....$17.95

BIG BOOK OF IRISH SONGS
76 songs.
00310981 ....$19.95

BIG BOOK OF ITALIAN FAVORITES
80 songs.
00311185 ....$19.95

BIG BOOK OF JAZZ
75 songs.
00311557 ....$19.95

BIG BOOK OF LATIN AMERICAN SONGS
89 songs.
00311562 ....$19.95

BIG BOOK OF LOVE SONGS
80 songs.
00310784 ....$19.95

BIG BOOK OF MOTOWN
84 songs.
00311061 ....$19.95

BIG BOOK OF MOVIE MUSIC
72 songs.
00311582 ....$19.95

BIG BOOK OF NOSTALGIA
158 songs.
00310004 ....$19.95

BIG BOOK OF OLDIES
73 songs.
00310756 ....$19.95

BIG BOOK OF RAGTIME PIANO
63 songs.
00311749 ....$19.95

BIG BOOK OF RHYTHM & BLUES
67 songs.
00310169 ....$19.95

BIG BOOK OF ROCK
78 songs.
00311566 ....$22.95

BIG BOOK OF SOUL
71 songs.
00310771 ....$19.95

BIG BOOK OF STANDARDS
86 songs.
00311667 ....$19.95

BIG BOOK OF SWING
84 songs.
00310359 ....$19.95

BIG BOOK OF TORCH SONGS
75 songs.
00310561 ....$19.95

BIG BOOK OF TV THEME SONGS
78 songs.
00310504 ....$19.95

BIG BOOK OF WEDDING MUSIC
77 songs.
00311567 ....$19.95